Stories in Motion

Vincent Weberink

<u>STORIES IN MOTION</u>

THE FILMMAKER ENTREPRENEUR

PZAZ, WHERE FILMS ARE MADE.

PZAZ

<u>Where Films Are Made.</u>

To all the filmmakers and creatives who navigate the chaos, fueled by passion and persistence.

"Creativity is the spark, but persistence is the fuel. In the chaos of creation, it's not just the art that matters—it's the journey."

Vincent Weberink

This book is a work of fiction. Names, characters, places, and incidents are products of the author's imagination. Any resemblance to actual events, locations, or persons, living or dead, is purely coincidental.

First paperback edition October 2024

Book design by Naim Has

ISBN 978-1-0685710-0-8 (Paperback)

CONTENTS

FOREWORD — IX

PREFACE — XII

INTRODUCTION — XV

1. THE ENTREPRENEURIAL CLUTTER — 1

2. PITCHING THE IMPOSSIBLE — 9

3. THE ART OF JUGGLING CHAOS — 18

4. MONEY TALKS, AND IT TALKS LOUD — 27

5. CREW CALAMITY   35

6. THE LONG NIGHT OF THE SOUL   48

7. REWRITING THE SCRIPT   57

8. LIGHTS, CAMERA, REDEMPTION   65

9. THE AFTERMATH   73

EPILOGUE   78

INTRODUCTION TO PZAZ   80

CHARACTER BIOGRAPHIES   84

ACKNOWLEDGMENTS   89

ABOUT THE AUTHOR   91

FOREWORD

As a filmmaker, I know firsthand the delicate balance between creativity and business. Every project is a juggling act—navigating budgets, managing teams, and dealing with the relentless pressures of deadlines, all while trying to stay true to your artistic vision. The Filmmaker Entrepreneur captures this reality in a way that is both insightful and entertaining.

This book is not just a guide for filmmakers; it's a candid exploration of what it really means to be an entrepreneur in the world of film. It highlights the highs, the lows, and the chaos that comes with turning ideas into something tangible while also offering solutions for how to stay afloat in an industry that demands as much from your business skills as it does from your creativity.

What makes this book stand out is its honesty. It doesn't sugarcoat the struggles—whether it's scrambling for funding, dealing with last-minute production issues, or handling the inevitable setbacks that occur during the creative process. But through it all, it reminds us why we do what we do: for the love of storytelling, the thrill of seeing our vision come to life connecting with the audience.

If you've ever wondered how to survive and thrive as a filmmaker, this book is a must-read. It's packed with wisdom, humour, and practical insights that will resonate with anyone who's ever picked up a camera—or even thought about it. More than that, it introduces Pzaz.io, a platform designed to help filmmakers manage the chaos of production, allowing them to focus on what truly matters: creating.

I wholeheartedly endorse The Filmmaker Entrepreneur for anyone who is passionate about filmmaking and entrepreneurship. It's not just a book—it's a roadmap for navigating the unpredictable, exhilarating world of film.

— Marianna Manta

PREFACE

As an innovator and entrepreneur, I've always been fascinated by industries that thrive on creativity and vision. The film industry, with its blend of artistry and business, captured my attention in a unique way. This book was born from that passion and a deep appreciation for the people who make films happen.

We wrote this fun little book to highlight the complicated lives of filmmakers—their struggles, their triumphs, and the challenges they face daily. Filmmaking isn't just about creating art; it's about managing tight budgets, coordinating large teams, navigating logistical headaches, and, most importantly, keeping the creative spark alive amidst all the chaos.

What makes this industry so captivating is that filmmakers are not just artists; they are entrepreneurs in their own right. They deal with the same pressures that startups and businesses face—except their product is often something deeply personal, a story they want to tell the world.

Throughout this book, you'll see the highs and lows of this unique journey. The challenges our characters face are the very ones that inspired the creation of Pzaz. It's a platform designed to support filmmakers in managing these complexities, helping them focus on their true passion—telling stories.

This book is a reflection of the dynamic, unpredictable nature of filmmaking. It's our way of showing just how much goes on behind the scenes, and how a little innovation can make a big difference in turning visions into reality. We hope it entertains, informs, and perhaps offers a glimpse into why we created Pzaz to make the filmmaker's life a little easier.

— Vincent Weberink

INTRODUCTION

This story follows Leif, a young, ambitious filmmaker whose passion often clashes with the industry's business side. Living in a dorm-like setup to keep his dreams alive, Leif is a creative visionary but struggles with the practicalities of film production. Alongside him is Inara, his pragmatic best friend who, while not a filmmaker herself, often plays the role of his unofficial assistant and voice of reason. Their dynamic captures the essence of the filmmaker's entrepreneurial journey—balancing art with the unrelenting demands of business.

Through Leif's journey, we illustrate filmmaking's highs, lows, and chaos, showing that success comes not just from creativity but from learning how to navigate the business side with grit and humour. Whether you're a filmmaker, entrepreneur, or both, this book offers insights, laughter, and a behind-the-scenes look at the trials that every creative mind faces.

At <u>Pzaz.io</u>, we've developed an ecosystem to help filmmakers manage the complexity of their daily lives and run their projects so that you can focus on what matters most: telling your story.

1

THE ENTREPRENEURIAL CLUTTER

Leif stared at the mountain of scripts, notes, and half-empty coffee cups covering his desk, wondering how his life had become such a mess. His dorm-like room—if you could call it that—was less of an office and more of a storage unit for abandoned projects and failed attempts at filmmaking. He had a vague idea of where things were, but "organized chaos" was the best way to describe his current state.

"How did I get here?" he muttered, picking up a crumpled script from the floor and tossing it into the growing pile of "maybe someday" projects.

His eyes landed on a worn-out film poster taped haphazardly to the wall. It was from his first student film —a low-budget, black-and-white, 22-minute short that had confused his professors more than inspired them. But it had been his first attempt, his first real project. That film lit the fire and made him believe filmmaking was his true calling. Now, a few years later, the dream was still alive, but so were the harsh realities that came with it.

He sighed, plopping down on his bed-turned-desk-chair. The rent was cheap in this rundown building, and it was the only place that allowed him to live on a tight budget while still pursuing his filmmaking dreams. It wasn't much, but it was his base of operations, and it would have to do for now.

The door creaked open, and Inara waltzed in, holding two cups of steaming coffee. She raised an eyebrow at the state of the room but said nothing, as she'd long since gotten used to the clutter.

"Morning, sunshine," she quipped, handing Leif a cup.

Leif took a sip, appreciating the caffeine hit. "You're late. I've already spiralled into my first existential crisis of the day."

"Only the first?" Inara replied with a grin. "Guess we're off to a good start."

Inara had been Leif's rock ever since film school. They had met in their first year, bonding over their shared frustration with the rigid expectations of their professors. They had spent countless nights ranting about the pretentiousness of the industry, promising each other that they'd break the mould and make films that mattered. Years later, Inara had taken a slightly different path—she was a digital artist with her own struggles, but she always seemed to have more of her life together than Leif did. Still, their friendship had only grown stronger.

Leif sank further into the worn cushions of the couch. "I've got a meeting with Tom to-day," he said, running a hand through his un-ruly hair. "Pitching the film to Mr. Sterling. Big-time investor."

Inara raised an eyebrow. "And you're not panicking?"

"Oh, I am," Leif replied, voice dripping with sarcasm. "I'm just doing it quietly so I don't freak out until later."

Inara chuckled. "Well, let's hope Sterling sees your genius."

Leif rubbed his temples, the weight of the pitch already pressing on him. It wasn't just the film he was pitching—it was his future. He had bills piling up, a dwindling bank account, and no backup plan. This investor meeting was make-or-break.

The conversation drifted to their time in film school, where the seeds of Leif's filmmaking dreams had first sprouted. They reminisced about late nights spent on set, using whatever resources they could scrape together to bring their student films to life. Leif had been so full of idealism back then, convinced that passion and hard work would be enough to break the industry's barriers.

But he had learned quickly that passion didn't pay the bills. The harsh realities of equipment costs, production schedules, and investor expectations had hit him hard. In those early days, he had laughed off the more business-oriented classes, thinking they didn't apply to "true artists." Now, as he stared at the budget spreadsheet he barely understood, he realised he should've paid more attention.

"How did I not get this before?" Leif muttered, half to himself.

Inara looked at him curiously. "Get what?"

Leif sighed, leaning back. "Film school. I thought it was all about art, storytelling, and vision. I didn't realise that I was also signing up for an MBA in film financing and production management."

Inara smirked. "Welcome to reality. You're basically running a startup, just with cameras and actors instead of apps and coders."

Leif took another sip of his coffee, thinking about how right she was. Filmmakers were entrepreneurs. He hadn't seen it at first, but it was painfully clear now that he was neck-deep in budgets and investor meetings. The dreams of artistic freedom had collided head-on with the practicalities of keeping a project afloat.

His phone buzzed with a message from Tom: Investor meeting in two hours. Be ready.

Leif sighed and put the phone back on the table.

"Guess it's time to go convince someone that I'm not just another starving artist," Leif said, standing up and stretching.

Inara gave him a supportive smile. "You'll be fine. Just don't lead with your 'this is art for art's sake' speech."

Leif laughed despite the growing anxiety gnawing at his gut. He grabbed his camera bag, keys, and the tattered notebook he used for all his brainstorming. As he stepped out into the hall, he glanced at the poster from his student film. The image that once represented idealism now seemed more like a reminder of how far he still had to go.

"Here we go," he whispered before heading out into the world of investors, budgets, and the relentless pursuit of a dream.

2

PITCHING THE
IMPOSSIBLE

Leif sat in the corner booth of a dimly lit café, nervously stirring his coffee as Tom arrived, looking as calm and collected as ever. The place was packed with aspiring creatives, the kind of people who spent their afternoons discussing grand ideas while barely scraping together enough money for rent. Leif knew them all too well—they were his tribe.

"So," Tom said, sliding into the booth across from Leif, "you ready for this?"

Leif gave a half-hearted shrug. "As ready as I'll ever be."

The meeting with Mr. Sterling was in less than an hour, and Leif was still trying to figure out how to present his film without sounding like a starry-eyed dreamer. He had rehearsed his pitch a dozen times, but whenever he imagined the conversation, he felt more like a salesman than a filmmaker. He glanced at his notebook, filled with scribbled ideas and disorganised budget numbers, wondering how he would make any of it sound professional.

Tom took a sip of his coffee and leaned back in the booth. "You know, this is just another pitch. You've done this before."

"Yeah, but not with someone like Sterling," Leif muttered. "This guy deals in millions, not thousands."

Tom chuckled. "Then just act like you're asking for millions. Confidence is key, my friend."

Leif tried to summon confidence, but all he could muster was the same pit in his stomach that had been growing for weeks. This wasn't just about getting funding for the film; it was about proving to himself and the world that he could do it.

The café was only a few blocks from Sterling's office, but the walk felt like a mile. As Leif and Tom entered the sleek downtown building, the polished marble floors and glass walls made Leif feel entirely out of place. He adjusted his jacket, suddenly aware of how outclassed he looked compared to the business professionals swarming the lobby.

They were escorted to a small conference room where Mr. Sterling was already waiting, impeccably dressed and reading something on his tablet. He barely glanced up as they entered.

"Mr. Sterling," Tom said with a smile, offering his hand. Sterling shook it briefly before gesturing for them to sit.

"So, what have you got for me?" Sterling said, cutting straight to the chase.

Leif felt his throat go dry. Tom shot him a glance, silently urging him to start the pitch. Leif took a deep breath and opened his notebook, trying to gather his thoughts.

"Well," Leif began, "the film is about connection—how people navigate relationships in a world that's more disconnected than ever."

Sterling looked up, raising an eyebrow. "Connection. Sounds a bit... conceptual. What's the commercial angle?"

Leif's mind scrambled. Commercial angle? He had always been so focused on the story, the art, that he hadn't thought much about how to sell it. Tom jumped in, sensing the struggle.

"We're aiming for a film that appeals to the art-house crowd but also has enough mainstream appeal to attract a wider audience," Tom explained. "Think Eternal Sunshine of the Spotless Mind meets Her."

Sterling leaned back in his chair, nodding slowly. "Alright. And what's the budget?"

Leif flipped to a page in his notebook, revealing a hastily scribbled budget that even he had trouble deciphering. He handed it over, praying that it looked professional enough.

Sterling scanned the page, his expression unreadable. After a long pause, he set the notebook down and folded his hands. "It's ambitious. But I like ambitious projects. That said, I'll need more than just passion. I need to know there's an audience out there willing to invest in this."

Leif blinked, unsure of what to say. "Invest?"

Sterling nodded. "Crowdfunding. I want to see if you can raise at least 30% of the budget through a crowdfunding campaign. If you can show me that there's a market for this, I'll match the rest."

Leif's heart sank. Crowdfunding? He hadn't even thought about that. His mind raced, trying to figure out how to pull off something like that, especially with so little time.

"We can do that," Tom said smoothly before Leif could object.

Sterling stood, signalling the end of the meeting. "Good. Get it done, and we'll talk."

Leif and Tom shook his hand and left the building, the weight of the new challenge settling over them.

As soon as they were outside, Leif turned to Tom, panic in his voice. "Crowdfunding? Seriously? How are we going to pull that off?"

Tom clapped him on the shoulder. "Relax. We'll figure it out. People love a good underdog story."

Leif wasn't so sure. He had spent so long trying to avoid turning this project into a popularity contest, but now he would have to sell it to the masses.

That night, Leif sat staring at his laptop screen in his apartment. He had already typed and deleted his crowdfunding pitch a dozen times, each version sounding worse than the last. He had watched other filmmakers run successful campaigns, but it always seemed like they had something he didn't—an easy confidence, a clear vision of what they wanted. Leif felt like he was still fumbling in the dark, trying to figure it all out.

He reached for his phone and texted Inara.

Leif: Crowdfunding. Sterling's idea. I'm toast.

Inara's reply came almost instantly.

Inara: Oof. How's the pitch going?

Leif: Awful. I sound like I'm begging for spare change on the subway.

Inara: Let me come over. We'll figure it out together.

Inara arrived half an hour later, armed with her laptop and a six-pack of cheap beer. She plopped beside Leif on the couch and pulled up a blank document.

"Alright," she said, cracking open a beer. "Let's get to work. We need something that sounds exciting but also relatable. You know, like you're not just asking for money—you're inviting people to be part of the journey."

Leif sighed, rubbing his temples. "Yeah, but it still feels like begging."

Inara smiled. "It's not begging if you're offering something of value. Remember that."

Leif took a deep breath, feeling a little more hopeful. With Inara's help, maybe he could pull this off. After all, filmmakers weren't just artists—they were entrepreneurs, and this was just another pitch—one of many he would have to make in his career.

8 3

THE ART OF JUGGLING CHAOS

The first day of pre-production was nothing short of pandemonium. Leif stood in the middle of the cramped space that served as their makeshift office, surrounded by a whirlwind of noise—phones ringing, people talking over each other, and the ever-present buzz of a crew that was just barely being held together by duct tape and hope. His head was spinning. Was this how real filmmakers worked? He had imagined it all differently—calmer, more organised, like one of those well-oiled machines you see in behind-the-scenes documentaries. Instead, it felt like he was in a tornado, trying to piece everything together on the fly.

Inara sat at the one functional desk in the room, rapidly typing away on her laptop. She glanced up at Leif and gave him a sympathetic smile. "You look like you're about to have a meltdown."

"I think I might be," Leif admitted, rubbing his eyes.

He had spent the better part of the week assembling a crew, but finding people willing to work on a shoestring budget wasn't easy. It was like herding cats—whenever he thought he had locked someone in, they'd slip away for a better-paying gig. It didn't help that most people willing to work with him were eccentric or inexperienced.

Their cinematographer, Jasper, was one of the few reliable ones. A quirky genius with an eye for detail, Jasper was known for working wonders with even the most limited equipment. Today, he was fussing over the lighting setup, muttering something about how the "vibe" wasn't quite right.

Inara's phone buzzed, pulling her attention back to the screen. "Bad news. Our actor for the lead role just bailed."

Leif's heart sank. "You're kidding."

Inara shook her head. "Apparently, they got a better offer. A paying offer."

Leif leaned against the wall, feeling the weight of the situation pressing down on him. He had poured everything into this project—his time, energy, and savings—and now it felt like everything was falling apart. They couldn't afford to lose more people. With the crowdfunding campaign just getting off the ground, every setback felt like another nail in the coffin.

"Well, we'll just have to find someone else," Leif said, trying to sound more confident than he felt.

The next few days were a blur of auditions, last-minute schedule changes, and frantic phone calls. Every time they took one step forward, something else seemed wrong. Their original filming location fell through, the sound guy quit because of a scheduling conflict, and they ran dangerously low on funds.

Leif was starting to wonder if he was in over his head. He had always known that filmmaking wasn't easy, but this? This was a whole new level of chaos.

"You're not the first filmmaker to go through this," Inara reminded him one evening as they sat on the apartment floor, sifting through potential cast photos.

"I know, but it feels like everything's falling apart," Leif said, leaning back against the couch. "This isn't how I imagined it would be."

"Yeah, well, nothing ever is," Inara said with a wry smile. "You've just got to roll with the punches. You'll figure it out."

The day of the auditions was both a disaster and a comedy show.

They had rented out a small, dingy room in a community centre for the casting call, and it quickly became apparent that things would not go as planned. The first actor to arrive was Kurt, a method actor who insisted on staying in character for the entire audition. The problem was that his "character" was some kind of mediaeval knight, complete with a fake British accent and a tendency to over-enunciate every word.

Leif exchanged a glance with Inara, who was doing her best to stifle her laughter as Kurt waved an imaginary sword and recited his lines with exaggerated bravado.

"Well, that was… something," Leif said after Kurt left, struggling to find the right words.

"Do you think we can hire him just for the entertainment value?" Inara joked, jotting down notes on her clipboard.

The next few auditions weren't much better. They had a Shakespearean-trained actor who insisted on delivering every line as though he were on stage at the Globe Theatre, a mime who communicated entirely in gestures, and a young actor who had misread the script and appeared in costume for an altogether different genre.

By the end of the day, Leif felt like his brain was fried. "We're doomed," he muttered, sinking into a folding chair.

Inara patted him on the shoulder. "Look on the bright side: at least it wasn't boring."

Just when Leif was about to throw in the towel, Jasper showed up with news that lifted everyone's spirits. "I found us a backup location," he announced, grinning from ear to ear.

"You're kidding," Leif said, jumping from his seat. "Where?"

Jasper leaned against the doorway, looking smug. "Old theatre downtown. It's not much, but I've got a friend who works there, and they're willing to let us shoot overnight, after hours."

Leif's relief was palpable. "That's perfect."

"Just one thing," Jasper added. "There's a ballet recital happening during the day, so we'll have to wait until they're done. But after that, it's all ours."

The realisation briefly tempered Leif's excitement that they would have to work around a bunch of tutu-clad kids, but at this point, he wouldn't complain. They had a location. They had a crew. They had a film to make.

When the night of the shoot finally arrived, it was predictably chaotic. They had to wait until the last of the ballet kids had cleared out, and by the time they were ready to shoot, everyone was exhausted. But as the cameras rolled and the scenes began to take shape, Leif felt a surge of energy. This was what it was all about—the late nights, the problem-solving, the creative breakthroughs. Even amidst the chaos, there was a certain kind of magic in the air.

As they wrapped up the night's shoot, Leif stood at the edge of the set, watching his crew pack up the equipment. It had been a long, exhausting day, but for the first time in weeks, he felt like they were actually moving forward.

"Not bad for a bunch of amateurs," Inara said, coming up beside him.

Leif smiled, his mind already buzzing with plans for the next day. "Yeah. Not bad at all."

4

MONEY TALKS, AND IT TALKS LOUD

Leif sat at his small kitchen table, staring at his laptop screen, scrolling through crowdfunding platforms. His head was still spinning from the meeting with Mr. Sterling. Crowdfunding had always seemed like a last resort, something desperate filmmakers did when all other options dried up. Now, it wasn't just an option—it was the only option.

The pressure was mounting. They needed to raise at least 30% of their budget from strangers on the internet, and Leif had no idea how to make that happen. He rubbed his temples, feeling the weight of the task.

"How do people even get strangers to care about their project?" Leif muttered to himself.

Inara, sitting on the couch with her laptop, looked up. "Well, the first step is convincing them that you're worth their money. And I hate to say it, but that means you're going to have to sell yourself."

Leif groaned. "I hate selling myself. I don't want to be one of those guys who's like, 'Please fund my project because it's art, and you need to support art!'"

Inara smirked. "Lucky for you, I'm here to make sure you don't sound like that. You just need a good story. People love stories."

Leif opened a blank document and started typing. He deleted the first few sentences almost immediately. It was more complicated than he thought to boil down his passion project into a neat little pitch that would appeal to both investors and film fans.

Over the next few days, Leif and Inara worked tirelessly to craft a crowdfunding campaign that was both compelling and authentic. Leif had never been good at self-promotion, but Inara relentlessly insisted they needed to put a personal touch on everything. She convinced him to record a short video introducing himself and explaining the project. The result was painfully awkward—Leif stumbling through his words, unsure how to convey his passion without sounding like he was begging.

"Don't worry," Inara said after they watched the footage. "We can edit the video to make you look less like a deer in headlights."

"Thanks," Leif said sarcastically. "That's exactly the kind of encouragement I needed."

The launch of the campaign was nerve-wracking. Leif checked his phone obsessively, waiting for the first donation to come in. Hours passed with nothing, and the sinking feeling in his stomach grew.

"What if no one donates?" Leif asked, pacing around the apartment. "What if this whole thing flops and we never get funding and—"

Inara held up a hand to stop him. "Leif, it's been, like, two hours. Chill."

But Leif couldn't chill. He had poured his heart into this project, and now it felt like he was asking the world to either validate his dream or crush it. The uncertainty was unbearable.

By the end of the first day, donations started trickling in—small amounts at first, mostly from friends and family. Leif wasn't sure if he should feel relieved or worried. Sure, it was a start, but they had a long way to go.

Then something unexpected happened. Someone posted about the campaign on a popular film blog, and suddenly, the donations picked up. Comments started flooding in from people Leif had never met, film fans who were excited by the concept and wanted to see the project succeed. It was surreal, watching strangers care about something that had once felt so personal, so small.

Leif stared at his laptop screen in disbelief. "People are actually interested."

Inara grinned. "Told you. It's all about the story."

As the days passed, the campaign continued to grow. Leif and Inara worked tirelessly, responding to comments, updating backers, and creating social media posts to keep the momentum going. The process was exhausting, but there was also a sense of excitement in the air—a feeling that maybe, just maybe, they could pull this off.

One night, his phone buzzed as Leif sat in front of his laptop. It was a message from Tom.

Tom: We're close to hitting our target. Sterling wants to talk next week.

Leif's heart raced. They were going to make it. He had been so focused on the day-to-day grind of the campaign that he hadn't allowed himself to believe it would succeed. Now, with the finish line in sight, the reality of the situation hit him. This was real. They were on the verge of making the film happen.

But along with the excitement came a new wave of anxiety. Once they had the money, there would be no turning back. They'd have to make the film—and it had to be good.

Inara, sensing his unease, glanced up from her laptop. "What's going on in that head of yours?"

Leif sighed, leaning back in his chair. "I'm freaking out."

"About what?"

"About everything," Leif admitted. "What if we mess this up? What if we get the funding and still fail?"

Inara closed her laptop and moved to sit beside him. "You won't fail. We won't fail. You've been busting your ass for this project, and now it's finally coming together. You're not alone in this. We've got a whole team, and we're all in this together."

Leif smiled weakly. "Thanks."

"Plus," Inara added with a smirk, "if you mess it up, I'll just make a documentary about that and call it a day."

Leif laughed, feeling some of the tension lift from his shoulders. He wasn't in this alone and didn't have to carry the weight of the entire project alone. They were all in it together, for better or worse.

As the campaign hit its target and the funds started rolling in, Leif and his team were one step closer to realising their dream. But the road ahead was still long, and the challenges were far from over.

5

CREW CALAMITY

Leif stood in the middle of the theatre-turned-set, staring at the controlled chaos surrounding him. It had taken weeks to get to this point, and now, on the first official day of shooting, everything seemed to be falling apart.

The theatre, which had looked so perfect during their late-night scouting visit, was now a hive of activity. Jasper mentioned that the kids' ballet recital was still in full swing and didn't look like it would end anytime soon.

Tiny dancers in tutus darted across the stage while frantic parents tried to corral them into something resembling order. Meanwhile, Leif's crew stood around awkwardly, waiting for their turn to take over the space.

"Are we shooting a documentary about chaos?" Inara quipped, standing beside Leif as they watched the scene unfold. "Because if we are, we've already nailed it."

Leif rubbed his temples, the stress mounting. "We'll just have to wait until they're done. Then we can reset and shoot overnight."

Inara raised an eyebrow. "Shoot overnight? Have you seen the crew? They're already half asleep."

Leif glanced at his team. Jasper was adjusting the camera, looking as unfazed as ever. The rest of the crew, however, looked less enthusiastic. A few of the grips were sitting on the floor, sipping coffee and yawning. The actors, who had been waiting for hours, were trying to stay in character, but their frustration was palpable.

"Look, I know it's not ideal, but we don't have a choice," Leif said. "We can't afford to lose this location."

Inara nodded, though her expression made it clear that she wasn't thrilled about the situation. "Alright. I'll make sure everyone's ready as soon as the recital wraps up."

Hours later, the last of the tiny ballerinas had finally cleared out, and Leif's crew sprang into action. They had less than six hours to shoot the first major scene, and everyone felt pressure. Jasper, ever the professional, started setting up the lighting while the rest of the crew scrambled to reset the stage for their shoot.

Leif ran through the scene in his head, making sure he hadn't missed any crucial details. It was a pivotal moment in the film—an emotional confrontation between the two lead characters, and Leif needed it to be perfect. But as the hours ticked by, and the exhaustion of the long day began to weigh on the crew, things started to go wrong.

First, one of the lights shorted out, casting strange shadows across the set. Jasper cursed under his breath as he tried to fix it, but the delay meant they were losing precious time. Then, one of the actors forgot his lines, stumbling over the dialogue as the rest of the cast and crew watched in painful silence.

Leif gritted his teeth, trying to keep his frustration in check. "It's fine," he said, more to himself than anyone else. "We'll just take it from the top."

But the night didn't get any easier. As they continued filming, more problems arose. Props went missing, the sound equipment malfunctioned, and tempers started to flare. By the time they wrapped the scene, it was well past 3 a.m., and Leif was on the verge of collapse.

The next day, Leif sat slumped at the small kitchen table in his apartment, his eyes heavy with exhaustion. Inara sat across from him, nursing a cup of coffee and scrolling through footage from the night before.

"Well, it's not terrible," Inara said, trying to sound optimistic.

Leif groaned, burying his face in his hands. "Not terrible? We had kids in tutus running around in half the shots."

Inara laughed. "Yeah, but that adds character."

Leif lifted his head and gave her a tired smile. "I'm starting to think this whole project is a disaster."

Inara shrugged. "Maybe. But you've survived disasters before. And look, we got the scene. It's rough, but we can work with it."

Leif sighed. She was right, as usual. The scene wasn't perfect, but they had gotten through it. And as much as he hated to admit it, there was something almost comforting about the chaos. It reminded him why he had gotten into filmmaking in the first place—not for the perfectly controlled sets or the polished Hollywood productions, but for the unpredictable, messy process of creating something from nothing.

"Alright," Leif said, standing up and stretching. "Let's keep going. One disaster at a time."

As the days went on, the crew continued to face challenge after challenge, but somehow, they managed to keep pushing forward. Each day brought new setbacks—lost locations, broken equipment, temperamental actors—but Leif and Inara found a rhythm in the madness. The more things went wrong, the more they learned to adapt, improvising solutions on the fly and leaning on each other for support.

Jasper, always calm under pressure, became the backbone of the crew. No matter what went wrong, he found a way to make the shots work, often turning technical glitches into creative opportunities. It wasn't ideal, but they were making progress. Slowly but surely, the film was taking shape.

One afternoon, as they were setting up for another shoot, Leif's phone buzzed with a notification. He glanced at the screen and saw an update from the crowdfunding campaign. They had surpassed their goal by 10%.

Leif blinked, hardly believing it. "We did it."

Inara looked up from her clipboard. "Did what?"

"The campaign," Leif said, grinning. "We hit our target. Actually, we went over."

Inara's eyes widened, and a smile spread across her face. "You're kidding. That's amazing!"

Leif felt a surge of relief wash over him. For the first time in months, he felt like they were going to pull this off. They had the funding, the crew, and—despite all the chaos—a film that was slowly coming together.

It wasn't perfect. In fact, it was far from it. But it was theirs, and that was enough.

Looking to Write Your First or Next Best-Seller?

~

~

Scan the QR Code!

6

THE LONG NIGHT OF THE SOUL

Leif sat on the edge of the bed in his small, cluttered apartment, staring blankly at the floor. His phone lay next to him, buzzing intermittently with messages he didn't feel like answering. The excitement of the crowdfunding campaign's success had worn off, and now the weight of everything still going wrong began to settle heavily on his shoulders.

They had been filming for weeks, and it felt like the setbacks were never-ending. Every day brought new problems—a malfunctioning camera, a missed location booking, a temperamental actor threatening to quit. And yet, through all of it, Leif had pushed forward, telling himself that it was all part of the process, that every filmmaker went through these challenges.

But tonight, it felt like too much.

Inara had gone home hours ago after another long day on set, and for the first time in a while, Leif was utterly alone. He had no more meetings to attend, no crew members to direct, no immediate fires to put out. All he had was the overwhelming sense of failure gnawing at him.

His mind wandered back to film school. The memories felt distant now, as if they belonged to someone else. Back then, he had been so optimistic, so sure that his passion for storytelling would carry him through whatever obstacles came his way. He had scoffed at the professors who tried to teach him about the business side of filmmaking. Budgets, timelines, investors—none mattered to him at the time. It was all about the art.

Now, he realised how naïve he had been.

The art wasn't enough. It had never been enough. Filmmaking wasn't just about telling stories—it was about building a business, managing people, navigating endless logistical nightmares, and somehow keeping the creative spark alive in the middle of it all.

And tonight, Leif wasn't sure if he had it in him anymore.

His phone buzzed again, and he glanced at the screen this time. It was a message from Tom.

Tom: Meeting with Sterling tomorrow. Need to finalise the budget.

Leif stared at the message, feeling a wave of anxiety rise in his chest. The meeting—he had almost forgotten. It was supposed to be the final step—securing the remaining funds from

Mr Sterling now that they had hit their crowd-funding goal. This was supposed to be the moment when everything finally came together. But instead of feeling relieved, Leif felt like he was entering another disaster.

What if they couldn't finalise the budget? What if Sterling decided to back out? What if, after all this time, the whole project fell apart?

He was exhausted—physically, mentally, emotionally. He had poured everything into this film, and now it felt like he had nothing left to give.

The following day, Leif dragged himself out of bed and made his way to the café where he was supposed to meet Tom. The air outside was crisp, and the sky was grey, matching Leif's mood. He strolled as if delaying the inevitable, but eventually, he reached the café and pushed open the door.

Tom was already there, sitting at a table with a stack of papers in front of him. He looked up as Leif approached, giving him a nod.

"You look like hell," Tom said, not unkindly.

"Thanks," Leif muttered, sinking into the chair across from him.

They spent the next hour reviewing the budget, fine-tuning the numbers and preparing for the meeting with Sterling. Leif tried to focus, but his mind kept drifting. The noise of the café, the clinking of cups and the low hum of conversation felt distant, like it was happening in another world. All he could think about was how much was riding on this meeting—on this film.

And he wasn't sure if he could handle it.

Later that night, as Leif sat alone in his apartment again, his phone buzzed with another message. This time, it was from Inara.

Inara: You alive?

Leif hesitated before responding. Barely.

A minute later, his phone buzzed again. Inara: Want me to come over?

Leif stared at the message for a long time before replying. Yeah.

When Inara arrived, she didn't say much at first. She sat down next to Leif on the couch, cracked open a beer can, and handed it to him. He took it without a word, grateful for the small gesture.

They sat silently for a while, the only sound being the occasional clink of their cans as they drank. Finally, Inara spoke.

"You know," she said quietly, "I've been thinking about what you said the other day. About how this whole thing feels like a disaster."

Leif glanced at her, waiting for her to continue.

"And I think you're right," Inara said with a smirk. "It is a disaster. But that's kind of the point, isn't it?"

Leif raised an eyebrow. "What do you mean?"

"I mean, that's what filmmaking is," Inara explained. "It's chaos. It's trying to wrangle a bunch of unpredictable people and unpredictable circumstances and somehow turn it into something coherent. Something beautiful. It's not supposed to be easy. And yeah, maybe we're in over our heads, but that's how you know you're doing something worth doing."

Leif considered her words, letting them sink in.

"I guess," he said, though his voice lacked conviction.

Inara nudged him with her elbow. "Hey. You've come this far. You're not quitting now, are you?"

Leif sighed, leaning back against the couch. "No. I'm not quitting."

"Good," Inara said, smiling. "Because I'd hate to have to finish this disaster without you."

Leif laughed despite himself, the tension in his chest easing just a little. He wasn't sure if things would get better or worse from here, but for the first time in days, he felt like maybe—just maybe—they could make it through.

7

REWRITING THE SCRIPT

Leif leaned back in his chair, staring at the chaotic whiteboard. Lines of dialogue, scene breakdowns, and character arcs were scrawled across the surface in a mess of colours, but none of it felt right. They had been shooting for weeks, but the film was starting to lose focus. And Leif was beginning to lose hope.

Tom and Jasper sat across from him, flipping through pages of the script, both looking equally tired. Inara paced the room, occasionally glancing at the board as if willing it to provide some kind of clarity.

"This isn't working," Leif said, finally breaking the silence. "The film's a mess. We're running out of time, out of money, and I don't even know if the story makes sense anymore."

Tom sighed, setting the script down. "We've hit a rough patch, yeah. But this is normal. Every film goes through it."

Leif shook his head. "No, it's more than that. I think we need to rethink the whole thing."

The others exchanged glances, unsure of what he meant.

"What are you suggesting?" Inara asked, stopping her pacing to face him.

Leif took a deep breath. "I've been thinki ng... Maybe we need to lean into the chaos. Everything's been going wrong since we started filming, and instead of fighting it, maybe we should embrace it."

Jasper tilted his head, intrigued. "What do you mean, 'embrace it'?"

"I mean, what if we turn this whole thing into a documentary? Not just about the story we're telling, but about the process—the behind-the-scenes madness of trying to make an indie film on a shoestring budget. The setbacks, the crew, the crowdfunding, all of it."

There was a pause as everyone considered the idea. Leif watched their faces, searching for a reaction. He knew it was risky—turning their project into a documentary would be a complete overhaul of what they had initially planned—but at this point, it felt like the only option.

Inara's lips slowly curled into a smile. "You know, that might actually be brilliant."

Tom chuckled. "It's definitely unconventional, but it's not the worst idea I've heard."

Jasper leaned back in his chair, arms crossed. "It's risky, but we've been shooting this thing guerrilla-style from the start anyway. We've already got some behind-the-scenes footage—why not build on that?"

Leif felt a surge of relief. They weren't shutting him down. In fact, they were starting to get excited about the idea. It wasn't the film they had set out to make, but maybe that didn't matter. Perhaps this new direction was what the project needed to survive.

The next few weeks were a whirlwind of rewrites, reshoots, and brainstorming sessions. Leif threw himself into the new direction, determined to make the documentary work. They restructured the entire project, shifting the focus from the fictional narrative they had started with to the real-life chaos of their production. The crew became part of the story, and the film evolved into a meta-commentary on the trials and tribulations of indie filmmaking.

As they shot more behind-the-scenes footage, capturing everything from technical mishaps to candid conversations about the creative process, Leif started to feel a renewed sense of purpose. This was what filmmaking was supposed to be about—adapting, evolving, and finding new ways to tell a story, even when everything seemed to be falling apart.

The crew rallied around the new direction, and despite the constant obstacles, there was a new energy on set. The actors, who had initially been sceptical of the shift, started to embrace their roles as themselves, adding a layer of authenticity to the project that Leif hadn't anticipated.

One night, as they wrapped a particularly chaotic shoot, Inara pulled Leif aside.

"I've got to hand it to you," she said, smiling. "This was a crazy idea, but I think it's actually working."

Leif grinned, though exhaustion was written all over his face. "Yeah, well, we'll see if anyone actually wants to watch a documentary about a film that never got made."

Inara punched him playfully on the arm. "Don't sell yourself short. People love a good underdog story. And that's exactly what this is."

Leif nodded, though the doubt still lingered. He wanted to believe her, but part of him was still terrified that the entire thing would crash and burn. The pressure of it all—trying to save a project that had been spiralling out of control—was almost too much to bear.

But for now, they were making progress. And that was more than he had hoped for a few weeks ago.

As they entered the final phase of filming, the documentary began to take shape in ways Leif hadn't expected. The story wasn't just about making a movie—it was about the struggles of every creative endeavour. It was about failure, perseverance, and finding meaning in the chaos.

And somehow, amidst all the setbacks and stress, Leif fell in love with the process again.

8

LIGHTS, CAMERA, REDEMPTION

The day of the film festival premiere had finally arrived, and Leif stood backstage, nerves jangling as the lights dimmed in the packed theatre. The crowd was buzzing with anticipation, but Leif wasn't sure if they were here to witness a success or a disaster. The documentary, now titled The Making of a Disaster, had taken on a life of its own in the indie film world, garnering attention for its candid portrayal of the chaos behind an underfunded, overambitious project.

Inara appeared beside him, giving him a reassuring nudge. "You look like you're about to puke."

"I might," Leif muttered, pulling at the collar of his shirt. His heart pounded in his chest, and he still struggled to believe they had finished the film—much less that people were eager to see it. It felt surreal, standing on the edge of what could either be a career-defining moment or a colossal failure.

"Relax," Inara said with a grin. "This is going to be great. Trust me."

Leif nodded, trying to calm his racing thoughts. He glanced over at Tom, sitting in the front row, looking as calm as ever, and Jasper, fiddling with a camera in the corner, ready to capture the audience's reactions. The crew had come a long way since their first disastrous shoot, and somehow, they had pulled it off.

As the lights dimmed further and the projector flickered to life, Leif's heart raced. The documentary's opening scenes played across the screen, showcasing the early days of the production—the auditions, the failed shoots, the endless setbacks. The audience chuckled at the absurdity of it all, and Leif found himself grinning despite his anxiety.

The film flowed from one disaster to the next, each moment more ridiculous than the last. But between the mishaps and missteps, there was a sense of heart and passion and people who cared deeply about what they were doing. As the film progressed, Leif realised that what they had created wasn't just a documentary about a failing production—it was a celebration of the creative process itself.

The audience laughed, leaning forward in their seats, wholly engaged in the story. As the final scenes played, showing the crew coming together to finish the project against all odds, Leif felt relief wash over him.

When the credits rolled, the theatre erupted into applause.

Leif blinked, momentarily stunned. He had expected polite claps at best, but this? This was overwhelming.

Inara grinned at him. "Told you."

Later that night, as Leif stood outside the theatre, mingling with the festival crowd, he was approached by a handful of industry professionals—distributors, critics, and filmmakers who had been blown away by the documentary's raw authenticity. They praised the film's honesty, its humour, and its heart, and Leif found himself receiving offers he never thought he'd hear.

"This is the kind of film we need more of," one producer said, shaking Leif's hand. "Something that shows the real struggles of indie filmmaking."

Leif smiled, the whirlwind of compliments and opportunities swirling around him. It was almost too much to process. A few months ago, he had been ready to quit, convinced that the entire project was doomed. And now, here he was, standing in the middle of a crowd that was celebrating the very chaos he had once feared would be his undoing.

As the night went on, Leif found himself alone on the theatre steps, taking a moment to breathe and reflect. The festival had been a success, the film was gaining traction, and for the first time in a long time, Leif felt he was exactly where he was meant to be.

Inara appeared beside him, holding two plastic cups of champagne. She handed one to Leif with a smirk. "So, what's next?"

Leif took a sip, staring out at the city lights. "I have no idea."

"Well, you better start thinking about it. People are going to be expecting more from you now. No pressure, though."

Leif laughed, the tension finally easing from his body. "Yeah, no pressure."

The next few weeks were a whirlwind of meetings, interviews, and discussions about future projects. The documentary had gone viral in the indie film community, and Leif found himself fielding offers from producers eager to collaborate with him on his next project. It was all happening so fast, and while part of him was exhilarated, another part was terrified.

But through it all, Leif felt a sense of purpose he hadn't felt in years. He had survived the film's chaos and was now ready for whatever came next. For the first time, he wasn't afraid of failure. He had learned to embrace the creative process's unpredictability, find beauty in the mess, and trust that even in the midst of disaster, something remarkable could emerge.

9

THE AFTERMATH

A month after the premiere, Leif was sitting in the same cramped apartment where it had all started. But now, everything felt different. His phone buzzed constantly with messages from producers, distributors, and collaborators who wanted to work with him. The film, The Making of a Disaster, had taken off in ways he never could have predicted.

Leif's life had shifted. No longer was he the struggling filmmaker scraping together funds and losing sleep over every slight mishap. Now, he was being asked to speak at panels, give interviews, and share his experience with audiences captivated by his story of turning chaos into art.

He still hadn't quite gotten used to the attention. Whenever someone approached him, praising the film's authenticity or humour, he couldn't help but feel a little out of place. But he was learning to accept that this was the new normal, at least for now.

As usual, Inara was by his side, helping him navigate his newfound success. She had always believed in the project, even when Leif had been ready to give up. Now, they sat together at a small café, going over plans for future projects.

"So, what's next?" Inara asked, sipping her coffee. "The world's waiting, you know."

Leif chuckled. "I'm still figuring that out."

In truth, he had a few ideas brewing in the back of his mind, but he wasn't in a rush. For the first time in years, Leif allowed himself to enjoy the moment. The grind of the last few months had been relentless, and he needed a break—just a little time to breathe before diving headfirst into the next project.

"Well, whatever it is, you know I'm in," Inara said with a grin.

Leif smiled. "I wouldn't want to do it without you."

The truth was, he couldn't imagine making a film without Inara by his side. She had been his rock throughout the entire process, grounding him when he spiralled and lifting him up when he doubted himself. Their partnership had grown stronger through the madness, and now, as they looked ahead to the future, Leif knew that they would face it together, whatever came next.

Later that day, Leif returned to his apartment, feeling a mix of excitement and trepidation. He sat down at his cluttered desk and opened his laptop, staring at the blank screen. Ideas for his next project were swirling in his head, but there was something else he needed to do first.

He opened a new document and began typing, the words flowing easily. It wasn't a script this time—it was a reflection. A letter to himself. A way of processing everything that had happened.

He wrote about their challenges, the moments when he had been ready to quit, and the small victories that had kept them going. He wrote about Inara, Tom, Jasper, and the crew who had stuck with him through thick and thin. And most of all, he wrote about how, in the end, it wasn't about perfection. It was about persistence. About pushing through the failures, embracing the chaos, and finding meaning in the mess.

When he finished, he leaned back in his chair, feeling a sense of peace. The journey wasn't over—far from it. But he had learned something valuable along the way.

Filmmaking wasn't just about telling stories. It was about survival, about adapting, about finding beauty in the unexpected.

And for the first time, Leif was ready for whatever came next.

EPILOGUE

Months after the success of The Making of a Disaster, Leif found himself on the set of his next film. The crew bustled around him, setting up cameras and lighting while actors rehearsed lines. It was chaos, as always, but Leif was at peace with it this time.

Standing beside him, Inara sipped her coffee, watching the organised frenzy with a smirk. "So, round two, huh?"

Leif grinned. "Round two."

The journey hadn't gotten any easier, but Leif had learned to embrace the madness. It was part of the process—part of what made filmmaking worth it. Every new project came with its own set of disasters, and Leif was ready for all of them.

As the camera rolled and the first scene began, Leif took a deep breath, watching his vision come to life once again. This time, the uncertainty didn't scare him. It excited him.

The future was still unpredictable, still messy, but Leif knew one thing for sure—he wasn't done telling stories. Not even close.

INTRODUCTION TO PZAZ

~

Pzaz was created with filmmakers in mind, understanding that the world of independent filmmaking is as much about entrepreneurship as it is about creativity. Filmmakers need to juggle numerous tasks: managing teams, budgets, schedules, and distribution while ensuring their vision is intact. Pzaz brings all these moving parts under one roof.

With Pzaz, you can:

- **Collaborate in Real-Time**: Whether you're working with your team across the street or across the globe, our real-time collaboration tools ensure everyone stays on the same page.

- **Script to Screen Workflow**: From script breakdowns to shot lists and storyboards, Pzaz keeps your creative process linked directly to your production needs.

- **Seamless Project Management**: Manage every aspect of your production, from scheduling to location management, with intuitive task lists and calendars.

- **Sync Across Departments**: Pzaz eliminates the barriers between creative and production teams by providing one platform that integrates every department's needs, reducing miscommunications and inefficiencies.

Unlike other project management tools, Pzaz is specifically tailored to filmmakers, providing features that cater to the unique demands of the film industry. This is not just another generic solution—this is a filmmaking ecosystem that empowers creatives to overcome the logistical hurdles that stand between them and their vision.

At Pzaz.io, we believe that every filmmaker deserves to focus on their craft, not the paperwork. That's why we've built Pzaz to be your all-in-one production hub, where creativity and efficiency meet. Let Pzaz handle the business, so you can focus on making your next masterpiece.

CHARACTER BIOGRAPHIES

Leif Olsen

Leif Olsen is a young, ambitious filmmaker with big dreams and a knack for navigating chaos. Fresh out of film school, Leif moved into a bare-bones apartment to save money while pursuing his creative passion. His journey as a filmmaker has been a whirlwind of setbacks, unexpected challenges, and learning to balance artistic vision with the realities of production. With a sharp sense of humour and a relentless drive, Leif turned his struggles into a celebrated documentary, The Making of a Disaster. Now, with newfound confidence, Leif continues to explore the world of independent filmmaking, embracing the entrepreneurial spirit that defines his career.

Inara Nilsen

Inara Nilsen is Leif's closest friend and creative partner, the voice of reason amidst the madness of film production. An artist in her own right, Inara shares Leif's frustrations with the ups and downs of the creative industry. Her practical approach and sharp wit have helped ground Leif when the pressures of filmmaking threaten to overwhelm him. Although she initially took on a behind-the-scenes role, Inara has become integral to Leif's projects, offering emotional support and logistical expertise. Her ability to balance creativity with pragmatism has made her invaluable to their team, and she continues to be a driving force behind their success.

Tom Rivera

Tom Rivera is Leif's producer and occasional therapist, the man who bridges the gap between Leif's artistic ambitions and the business side of filmmaking. With years of experience navigating the world of film financing, budgeting, and pitching, Tom has been a steady hand in the storm of Leif's projects. Though his calm demeanour often masks the chaos around him, Tom knows how to get things done and profoundly respects the passion that drives filmmakers like Leif. Tom's expertise has helped guide Leif through the numerous obstacles of independent filmmaking, and his belief in the project has been key to its success.

Jasper Crowley

Jasper Crowley is the eccentric, talented cinematographer who worked closely with Leif on The Making of a Disaster. Known for his ability to create stunning visuals with limited resources, Jasper brought an artistic flair to the project that helped elevate it from a simple behind-the-scenes documentary to a visually compelling narrative. With his laid-back attitude and creative problem-solving skills, Jasper became the go-to guy for making things work when everything seemed to be falling apart.

His unique style and dedication to his craft continue to make him a sought-after collaborator in the indie film scene.

ACKNOWLEDGMENTS

Creating this little book has been a true team effort, and I'm incredibly grateful to everyone who contributed to its completion.

First, a big thank you to Naim for bringing the book to life with his stunning cover design and graphics. Marianna Manta, your sharp eye and expertise in filmmaker facts ensured our story stayed grounded in reality. Sotiris Alexandrakis and Bruno Cepele, your tireless work in promoting the book has been invaluable. Efthymia Efstathiou, thank you for helping Hypno to take his first selfie. Ben Cena, your unwavering support was essential to making this publication happen.

To my lovely wife Monique, whose wisdom shapes my journey—I couldn't have done any of this without you.

Finally, thank you to the entire Pzaz team for your dedication and hard work. This is the first one of what I hope will be a series of books about the film maker entrepreneur, and I'm proud to have you all by my side as we embark on this exciting journey together.

ABOUT THE AUTHOR

Vincent Weberink is an experienced startup and growth strategist, technologist, and innovator with a knack for turning products upside down and creating disruptive solutions. Having lived and worked in over seven countries, he has gained unique insights into diverse cultures and markets. Vincent is the founder of Pzaz.io, a platform that supports filmmakers who blend creative vision with entrepreneurial ambition. Working closely with his team at Pzaz, he co-created *The Filmmaker Entrepreneur*, a book that humorously and insightfully highlights the real-world challenges filmmakers face, from managing tight budgets to navigating logistical chaos.

Vincent's journey in business has led him to specialize in product management, strategy, and innovation. His son, Benjamin Weberink, a talented young writer and author of *The Fatal Stillness of the Sun*, continues the family's creative legacy.

www.ingramcontent.com/pod-product-compliance
Lightning Source LLC
Chambersburg PA
CBHW031311060726
47590CB00003B/1165